D1630194

STAR WARS

EPISODE I

Who's Who

STAR WARS

EPISODE I™

Who's Who

by Ryder Windham

Running Press
PHILADELPHIA • LONDON

A Running Press Miniature Edition™

© 1999 Lucasfilm Ltd. & ™. All rights reserved. Used under authorization.

Printed in China

Library of Congress Cataloging-in-Publication Number 98-67642

ISBN 0-7624-0728-X

Running Press Book Publishers
125 South Twenty-second Street
Philadelphia, Pennsylvania 19103-4399

Visit us on the web!
www.runningpress.com

Introduction

Months before the theatrical premiere of *The Empire Strikes Back*, *Star Wars* was rereleased with the subtitle Episode IV: *A New Hope*. This apparent revision prompted much speculation about the unproduced preceding episodes in the *Star Wars* saga.

Asked about his overall concept of *Star Wars* in a 1979 interview, George Lucas stated, "Originally, when I wrote *Star Wars*, it developed into an epic on the scale of *War and Peace*, so big I couldn't possibly make it into a movie. So I cut it in half, but it was still too big, so I cut each half into three parts. I then had enough material for six movies." Lucas added that the first trilogy would be about the young Obi-Wan Kenobi and the early life of Luke Skywalker's father.

In the years following *Return of the Jedi*, the adventures of Luke Skywalker only grew more popular. In numerous novels, comic books and games, the epic struggle between the Empire and the Alliance continued far beyond the Battle of Endor. Seldom did these stories venture before the events of *A New Hope*, however, and with good reason: that period was reserved for George Lucas.

When Lucas began scripting Episode I, fans wondered anew if any other familiar characters would be featured in the new film. Audiences will be delighted to see that Anthony Daniels, Frank Oz, and Kenny Baker have returned to their respective roles as C-3PO, Yoda, and R2-D2. Ian McDiarmid appears without heavy makeup to reprise his performance as Palpatine, the man who will be Emperor. A younger Jabba the Hutt also has a welcome cameo. Best of all, George Lucas was again in the director's chair for all of it.

There are many new characters, and most are represented in this book. Some may appear minor, but you never know who might affect the fate of the galaxy. Rest assured. As with the other *Star Wars* films, Episode I will inspire and entertain audiences for generations to come.

SUPREME CHANCELLO VALORUM

Responding to the Trade Federation's blockade of the Sovereign system of Naboo, **Supreme Chancellor Valorum** of the Galactic Republic sends two ambassadors to settle the matter diplomatically. Valorum does not inform the Neimoidians that both ambassadors are Jedi.

An accomplished Jedi Knight, **Qui-Gon Jinn** is closely attuned to the living Force. Regarded as something of a maverick by the Jedi Council, the middle-aged Qui-Gon remains an active, powerful warrior. Qui-Gon's empathy for other living things is perhaps his greatest strength.

QUI-GON

OBI-WAN

The apprentice to Qui-Gon Jinn, **Obi-Wan Kenobi** accompanies his mentor on the diplomatic mission to Naboo. Although Obi-Wan greatly respects and admires Qui-Gon, he is bewildered by his elder's tendency to take other life forms under his wing. In the future, Obi-Wan himself will attempt teaching the ways of the Force to a young apprentice, unaware that his effort will result in devastating consequences for the entire galaxy.

KENOBI

RUNE

A lieutenant with the Trade Federation, **Rune Haako** oversees the invasion of the peaceful planet of Naboo. Realizing that the two ambassadors who boarded the immense Trade Federation battleship are really Jedi, Rune Haako warns his viceroy, Nute Gunray.

NUTE GUNRAY

Seemingly in charge of the Trade
Federation's invasion of Naboo,
the Neimoidian Viceroy **Nute Gunray**
is actually carrying out the transmitted
orders of Darth Sidious, a Sith Lord.
Commanded by Darth Sidious to
kill the two Jedi, Nute Gunray soon
realizes this is a nearly impossible task.

The Sith Lord **Darth Sidious** is the true mastermind behind the Trade Federation's aggressive tactics. Orchestrating the conquest of Naboo from a remote location, Darth Sidious also has sinister designs against Queen Amidala.

DARTH

Amidala

The recently elected leader of Naboo, **Queen Amidala** rules from the city of Theed. Deeply committed to her people, she hopes to achieve a nonviolent resolution in the face of the Trade Federation's invasion.

PALPATINE

Representing Naboo at the Galactic Senate, the well-respected **Senator Palpatine** is pleased when the Queen agrees to meet him on Coruscant. However, Palpatine cautions the Queen that Naboo may not receive any genuine support from Supreme Chancellor Valorum.

SIO BIBBLE

Governor of Theed, the forthright
Sio Bibble remains on Naboo during
the Trade Federation's occupation
of the planet.

Dedicated to the safety of Queen Amidala, **Captain Panaka** heads the Naboo Royal Security Forces. Knowing his small team cannot defend against a planetary assault, Panaka agrees to accompany the Queen to Coruscant, where she can appeal to the Galactic Senate.

An unfortunate outcast from Naboo's underwater city Otoh Gunga, **Jar Jar Binks** is rescued by Qui-Gon from the Trade Federation's attack. Hoping to escape from the invading forces, the amphibious Gungan reluctantly leads Qui-Gon and Obi-Wan to Otoh Gunga, even though it means he'll have to face the unforgiving Boss Nass.

Leader of the Gungans, **Boss Nass**
banished Jar Jar Binks from Otoh Gunga
for his part in a clumsy accident.
Lumbering and heavyset, the surprisingly
perceptive Boss Nass remains an
intimidating figure among his people.
Qui-Gon Jinn manages to persuade Boss
Nass to spare Jar Jar's life, allowing
Jar Jar to help the Jedi find Queen Amidala.

Introduced as Queen Amidala's most trusted handmaiden, **Padmé** joins the Queen, Captain Panaka, Ric Olié, Jar Jar Binks and the two Jedi in their flight from Naboo.

PADMÉ
NABERRIE

A native of Naboo, **Ric Olié** pilots space-craft for the Naboo volunteer security forces. Flying the unarmed Naboo royal starship, Olie helps Queen Amidala and her small entourage escape Naboo during the Trade Federation's invasion.

Several astromech droids serve
Queen Amidala's royal starship.
When the ship is attacked by Trade
Federation battleships, the astromech
R2-D2 responds with quick efficiency
and daring action. Queen Amidala
herself cannot help but be impressed
by the plucky droid's bravery.

When Darth Sidious learns that Queen
Amidala has escaped from Naboo,
the Sith Lord sends his loyal apprentice
Darth Maul to track her down. A fierce
warrior, Maul strikes fear into all who
see his menacing, broadly tattooed
face. Shrouded in mystery, Darth Maul
appears possessed by the dark side
of the Force.

The Toydarian proprietor of a Mos
Espa junk shop on the planet Tatooine,
Watto is also an incorrigible gambler
who enjoys wagering on high-speed
Podraces. A bet with Gardulla the Hutt
resulted in Watto's acquisition of
the slaves Anakin and Shmi Skywalker.
Much to Qui-Gon Jinn's surprise and
dismay, Toydarians are immune to Jedi
mind tricks.

WATTO

ANAKIN

Despite his status as a slave, young **Anakin Skywalker** enjoys a reputation in Mos Espa as the only human capable of flying a Podracer. His quick reflexes are matched by astonishing piloting skills beyond his years. After Queen Amidala's spacecraft lands for repairs on Tatooine, Anakin's life is forever changed by a fateful meeting with Qui-Gon Jinn.

Widely regarded as the best Podracer in Mos Espa, **Sebulba** is also the most feared. An arboreal Dug, Sebulba's dexterous feet serve as his manipulatory appendages. The only thing that delights Sebulba more than winning a Podrace is watching the demise of another racer.

SEBULBA

SHMI

A slave owned by the junk dealer Watto, Anakin's mother **Shmi Skywalker** is bound, like all slaves, by an electronic implant that prevents escape. Hoping to free both Shmi and Anakin, Qui-Gon is only able to bargain Anakin's freedom from Watto. Although Shmi is heart-broken to lose her son, she senses Anakin's destiny is with the Jedi.

Displaying a high aptitude with technology, Anakin uses spare parts to construct a protocol droid named **C-3PO**. Anakin hopes the unfinished droid will help his mother and watch over her after he leaves Tatooine. When C-3PO first meets the astromech R2-D2, neither droid has any idea that their destinies will one day become entwined.

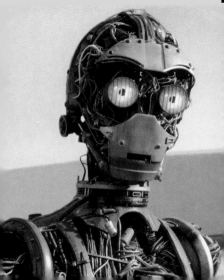

JABBA HUTT

In the years to come, the corpulent megalomaniac **Jabba** will eliminate most of his competition in the Outer Rim Territories, gaining increasingly infamous notoriety for his spice dealing, slave trading, and employment of bounty hunters. Accompanied by his entourage, Jabba hosts the Boonta Eve Podrace from his personal spectator platform.

The dashing playboy **Wan Sandage** has been racing Podracers since he was two years old. Now six, the aging Devlikk knows his only chance of winning the Boonta Eve Podrace is to get rid of Sebulba. Realizing he can't do it alone, Sandage enlists the services of fellow racer Aldar Beedo.

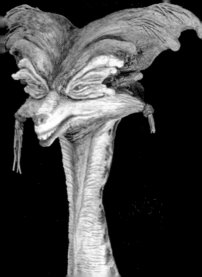

ALDA

Recently returned from a successful assignment in the Ploo Sector, the Glymphid hitman **Aldar Beedo** is a second-rate Podracer. He is less interested in winning the Podrace than in Wan Sandage's considerable cash advance to terminate Sebulba.

BEEDO

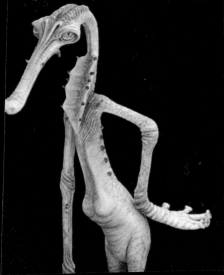

After nearly being overtaken by Anakin Skywalker in a previous Podrace, **Ark "Bumpy" Roose** views the young human as a threat. Intending to disable Anakin's Podracer controls, the dim-witted Roose mistakenly tampers with Ben Quadinaros' Podracer instead.

ROOSE

BEN QUADINAROS

Short by Toong standards, the affable **Ben Quadinaros** is the tallest entrant in the Boonta Eve Podrace. Entirely inexperienced, Quadinaros' hastily built Podracer never makes it past the starting line, but he still profits greatly from his bet with Boles Roor.

A reeking Sneevel, the notoriously wealthy glimmik singer **Boles Roor** was performing at a crowded Mos Espa casino when he began taunting a timid Toong from the stage. Drunkenly wagering five million peggats that Toongs were too cowardly to enter a Podrace, Boles Roor was chagrined when Ben Quadinaros took the bet.

Reining the longest pair of engines in the Boonta Eve Podrace, the Veknoid outcast **Teemto Pagalies** secretly pines for Ann Gella, one of Sebulba's Twi'lek masseuses. Believing that fellow Podracer Mars Guo intends to abduct Ann Gella, Pagalies cautiously alerts Sebulba.

A Phuii and relentless braggart, **Mars Guo** barely remembers the glimmik concert or his vacuous offer to take Ann Gella away from Tatooine. Trying to focus and prepare for the Podrace, the bleary-eyed Guo doesn't notice Sebulba dropping a small bit of metal in the Phuii's right engine.

GUO

DUD

An unscrupulous toady, the Vulptereen
Podracer **Dud Bolt** is secretly paid
by Sebulba to be the Dug's mid-air
bodyguard. Dud Bolt receives a bonus
for any Podracer he brings down.

BOLT

GASGANO

Although the twenty-four-fingered Xexto has never beaten Sebulba, **Gasgano** is a popular favorite in the Boonta Eve Podrace. Racing on behalf of Gardulla the Hutt, Gasgano is the subject of frenzied betting between Gardulla and Jabba.

Born on Tatooine, **Ody Mandrell** has an insatiable appetite for high-speed thrills. With little respect for any life form, Ody is a reckless menace on the Podrace course.

ODY
MANDRELL

CLEGG
HOLDFAST

A participatory journalist for *Podracing Quarterly*, **Clegg Holdfast** is regarded as something of a joke among other Podracers. Holdfast's writing is infinitely better than his Podracing skills.

After placing first in three consecutive semi-pro Podracing tournaments on the planet Malastare, **Ebe Endocott** spent his winnings on a new Corellian freighter to carry him and his Podracer to Tatooine. A confident Triffian, Ebe believes Sebulba's winning days are over.

ENDOCOTT

An amphibian from the Ploo Sector, Kam Nale entered the Boonta Eve Podrace under the name **"Elan Mak"** to conceal his true identity. The son of a recently murdered Fluggrian crime lord, Kam Nale intends to kill his father's assassin: Aldar Beedo.

MAK

MACE

A Senior Jedi on the twelve-member Jedi Council, **Mace Windu** believes the Sith are extinct. He is astonished when Qui-Gon recounts the battle with Darth Maul on Tatooine.

WINDU

One of the only Knights to serve on the Jedi Council, **Ki-Adi-Mundi**, like all Cereans, has a binary brain. This attribute allows him unique insight into the dark side of the Force.

MUNDI

The daughter of Corellian diplomats on Coruscant, Jedi Master **Adi Gallia** was the first to warn Chancellor Valorum of the probable invasion of Naboo by the Trade Federation.

GALLIA

After her emigrating family was slain by space pirates, the six-month-old **Depa Billaba** was rescued by Mace Windu. Sensing the infant's strength in the Force, Mace Windu brought her to Coruscant for training. Now a Jedi Master, Depa Billaba is one of the most recent additions to the Council.

EETH

A Zabrak born in the violent slums of
Nar Shaddaa, Jedi Master **Eeth Koth**
sees something of himself in the scruffy
Anakin Skywalker. At the age of four,
Eeth had also been deemed too old
to begin Jedi training, but he had the
advantage of Zabrak thought control.

KOTH

RANCISIS

Disavowing his inherited title, Monarch of Thisspias, Jedi Master **Oppo Rancisis** is a cunning military strategist. Oppo devised the tactics that allowed the Jedi to win many space battles.

Steadfastly refusing a prosthetic
replacement for the eye he lost
in combat against seven terrorists,
Jedi Master **Even Piell** reveals
his heritage as a Lannik warrior.
Piell wears the scar as badge
of honor, a reminder that it was
he who survived the battle.

A courageous fighter, **Plo Koon** comes from a long line of Jedi. Having fought with Qui-Gon Jinn in previous conflicts, he hopes Qui-Gon will one day join him on the Jedi Council.

KOON

SAESEE TIIN

Born on the moon Iktotch, Jedi Master **Saesee Tiin** augments his Force powers with the natural telepathic ability of the Iktotchi. A daring starpilot, he single-handedly disabled three battleships.

Of the same species as Yoda, Jedi Master **Yaddle** is highly regarded for her wisdom, patience and compassion.

YADDLE

YARAEL

An invertebrate native of Quermia, Jedi Master **Yarael Poof** is legendary for his skills at mind effects. In battle, his dynamic mental conjurings have convinced the most violent enemies to surrender.

LOTT DOD

The Senator for the Trade Federation,
Lott Dod denies any wrong doing on
the part of the Neimoidians on Naboo.

PRINCE
BAIL

Prominent senator to the Republic
from Alderaan, **Prince Bail Antilles**
is a nominee to succeed Valorum
as Supreme Chancellor.

ANTILLES

Sitting beside Mace Windu on the Jedi Council, wise Master Yoda is vocal in his opposition to Qui-Gon's request to train Anakin as a Jedi Knight. Decades later, **Yoda** will recall this time as perhaps the most pivotal moment in the history of the galaxy.

YODA

This book has been bound using handcraft methods and Smyth-sewn to ensure durability.

The dust jacket and interior were designed by Corinda Cook

All film stills and photographic materials are from the Lucasfilm Archives, coordinated by Tina Mills

The text was edited by Marc Frey and Allan Kausch

The text was set in Eurostile and Flexure